What is a Honeybee?

Like all insects, honeybees have six legs and three body sections – the head, thorax and abdomen. But honeybees are very different from wasps and hornets. Besides their shape, honeybees are also different in that they make and store honey, build nests from wax instead of paper, eat pollen and nectar instead of other insects, and can sting only one time.

THE BUZZ
During the summer months, honeybees store honey inside the hive to eat when winter arrives.

Apis florea (Dwarf Honeybee)

Apis dorsata (Giant Honeybee)

Apis mellifera (Common Honeybee)

Apis laboriosa (Himalayan Honeybee)

Apis cerana (Indian Honeybee)

Bumblebee or Honeybee?

Like honeybees, bumblebees eat nectar and gather pollen, but they are different than honeybees in several ways. Bumblebees are larger and furrier-looking than honeybees. Bumblebee queens actually go out and collect food and build the nests, whereas honeybee queens only lay eggs. Their stinger is different, too, allowing bumblebees to sting more than just one time.

Friends of the Earth

Do you like to eat blueberries, strawberries, almonds, apples, carrots and pears? You can thank honeybees for these and other delicious foods. About one-third of the foods we eat are pollinated by honeybees.

When a bee lands on a flower, pollen sticks to its legs and gets passed from flower to flower with each visit the bee makes. That is how many plants reproduce.

Honeybees also pollinate food for cows, sheep and other livestock whose milk or meat people eat. They pollinate cotton plants too... so even our clothes are dependent on honeybees.

THE BUZZ
Honeybees can fly 10 - 15 mph and will visit up to 100 flowers in one trip.

Beekeeping

Some people keep their own bee colonies to make honey and use the wax. Many of these beekeepers lend their bees out to farmers. They'll drive from southern California all the way up to Canada letting their bees pollinate a farmer's crops. The bees fly about the farmland or orchard and when they're done, return to the hive. Then the beekeeper drives up to the next place. Every year farmers use tens of billions of bees to help them out.

It would be very difficult to carry around beehives, let alone reaching inside to gather the honey. So, beekeepers make frames for their hives out of wooden boards. Each hive usually has ten frames, in the shape of a box. There is just enough spacing in between the boards for the bees to move easily between the frames. The bees usually raise their young in the bottom section, and store honey in the top sections.

When it comes time to get the honey out of the hive, the beekeepers pull out one frame at a time and use a special hot knife blade to uncap each cell that the bees have sealed. Then the beekeeper pours the honey out of the cells and fills the jar with fresh, sticky honey.

Beekeeper and boxed hives

THE BUZZ
Did you know that honey never spoils? Bacteria can't grow in honey.

A Peek Inside The Hive

Wild honeybees make their hives in holes in trees, rocks, and inside caves. A hive is made up of many perfectly-shaped, six-sided cells. The worker bees form these cells out of wax made by their own bodies.

THE BUZZ
Bees also collect sticky sap from trees and use it to glue and repair the sides of the hive.

THE BUZZ
Honeybees bring nectar into the hive and place it in the honeycomb's six-sided cells. Then they fan it with their wings, turning it into thick honey.

Honeycomb cells

Who's Who?

A honeybee colony can be huge, often having 60,000 members. The colony is made up of three different kinds of honeybees: the queen, workers, and drones.

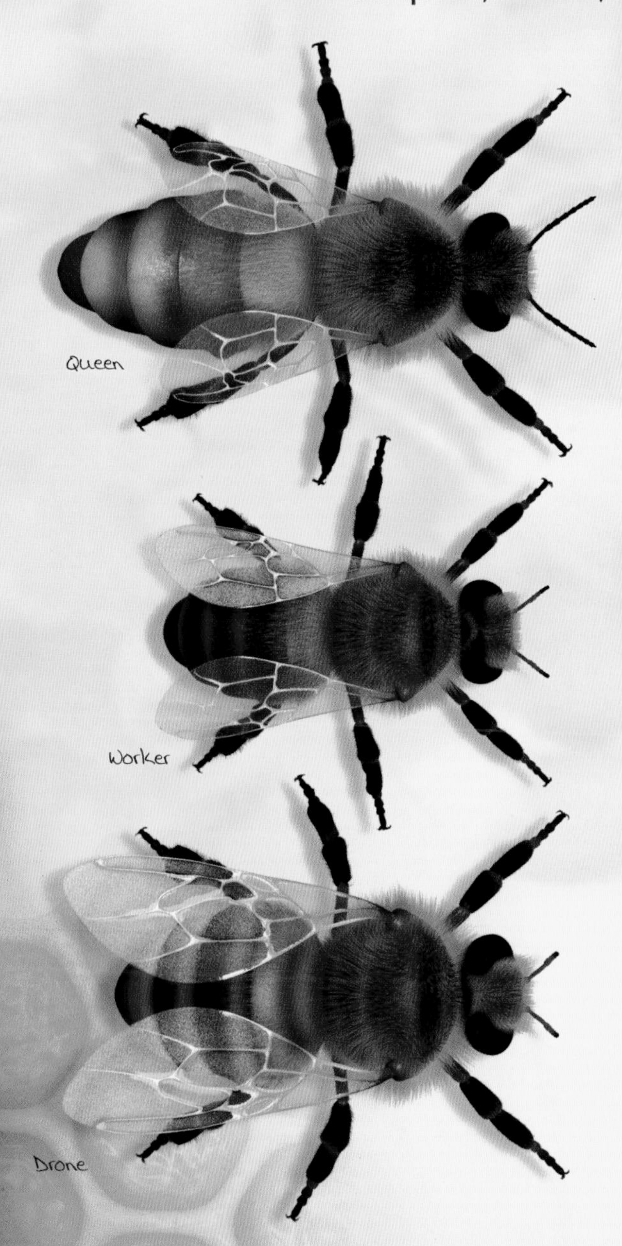

Queen

Each colony has only one queen. Her only job is to lay eggs. She can lay as many as 2,000 eggs a day. Queens usually live 2 - 3 years.

Workers

The thousands of workers in a colony are all females and are very busy bees! They do many jobs in and out of the hive. They collect nectar and pollen, clean and build the hive, store honey, guard the hive, feed the queen and larvae, make wax, and raise and lower the temperature in the hive.

Drones

Each colony has about 100 drones, which are all males. Their only job is to mate with the queen. They will do this just once and then die after mating.

From Egg to Bee

Honeybees begin their lives as tiny eggs. The queen places one tiny egg in each cell of the honeycomb. The eggs become larvae, which look like little worms. All they do is eat before spinning their cocoons. Worker bees bring food to the larvae. They make a special food called royal jelly that they give to the queen larvae. That helps her grow bigger and stronger than the others. Within less than two weeks, the eggs have become honeybees. This change is called metamorphosis.

Swarming

What happens when a hive gets too crowded? It's time to go house hunting. This usually happens in late spring. Worker bees eat their fill of honey and then spend their time looking for a new place to build a new hive. Once they find a good location, they wiggle their body and move in a specific direction to tell others where it is. Then about half the workers and the queen form a swarm and move to this location. A few days later, a new queen emerges in the old hive and takes over as the queen bee.

So You Think You Can Dance?

Bees don't talk, but they sure know how to communicate with each other. They do this by dancing! After a bee has been out and about, it'll come back to the nest to let the others know where the best flowers are. Just like the dance they do to let others know where a good location for the new hive is, it's all communicated inside the hive in total darkness.

Waggle dance

A worker bee will move in a sort of figure eight shape. The dance shows direction, distance, how much food there is and how good it is. A faster, stronger dance means a better food source.

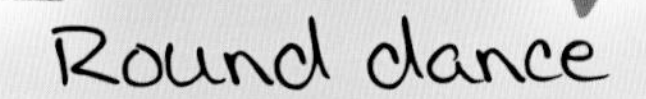

A worker bee will dance in a circle if the source is not that far away. This dance doesn't show exact direction like the waggle dance does, but communicates the smell of a good food source.

THE BUZZ
Only female honeybees sting. They will sting if they feel that their hive is in danger. It's not something they really like to do, because they die after they sting.

THE BUZZ
No matter what the temperature is outside, honeybees keep the inside of their nest at a steady 92 - 93 °F.

Disappearing Bees

Honeybees face many threats during the year. They can get eaten by birds and other animals, or get a number of diseases. A few years ago, scientists noticed that thousands of honeybees were dying. They flew out of their hives to collect nectar and pollen, but didn't return as usual. Scientists believe that it could be a virus that is causing them to die off at a faster rate than in the past. They call this colony collapse. Many people are working very hard to solve this mystery and help save the honeybees.

HONEYBEES